James Bunting was born and raised in Bristol. He started writing aged 13 and doing nothing with his poems until, at 18, a chance encounter with three American performance poets introduced him to a style of poetry that proved the jump-start for his writing. Since that night, James has performed extensively throughout the UK, including at literature festivals, music festivals and slams alongside some inspirational poets. His writing has been described as powerful and emotive, and his performances regularly leave audiences in awed silence. Conkers is his debut collection and features many of the poems that have taken him across the country over the past eight years. James now lives in London and works in PR.

Conkers

James Bunting

Burning Eye

BurningEyeBooks
Never Knowingly
Mainstream

Copyright © 2016 James Bunting

The author asserts the moral right under the Copyright, Designs and Patents Act 1988 to be identified as the author of this work.

All rights reserved. No part of this publication may be reproduced, stored in a retrieval system, or transmitted, in any form or by any means without the prior written consent of the author, nor be otherwise circulated in any form of binding or cover other than that in which it is published and without a similar condition being imposed on the subsequent purchaser.

This edition published by Burning Eye Books 2016

www.burningeye.co.uk
@burningeyebooks

Burning Eye Books
15 West Hill, Portishead, BS20 6LG

ISBN 978-1-909136-89-2

Conkers

CONTENTS

IMMORTAL	13
SARANGNI	15
BONES	16
CONKERS	19
DOG	21
STORMS	23
SHIPPING	25
CATHY	27
EINAUDI	30
HOME	31
UNTITLED	32
PUPPET	33
BRISTOL	34
INSOMNIA	36
ONCE	38
GRAFFITI	39
KETTLE	42
FOXES	43
FOOL	44
LONELY	46
FOOTPRINTS	47
DYLANS	48
WRITE	50
SENSE	52
JULY	53
PHOTOGRAPHS	54

For all my sins…

A poet is a poet for such a very tiny bit of his life; for the rest, he is a human being, one of whose responsibilities is to know and feel, as much as he can, all that is moving around and within him, so that his poetry, when he comes to write it, can be his attempt at an expression of the summit of man's experience on this very peculiar and this apparently hell-bent earth.

– Dylan Thomas

IMMORTAL

The Hindu sages say that of all the world's miracles the greatest miracle is that even though we know we are mortal
we live as if we are immortal.

It must be the worst realisation to wake one day and say this bag of heart, love, lust and bones, will one day cease to be anything but a memory — to say this day is one day ticked off the total. I will never get this day back.

Jonny thought that he would live forever, so he did as he pleased. He kissed, he ran, swang, and he missed. He would reach down this throat to turn himself inside out then laugh. If you ever meet a man so wrought with his own sense of self that he can change history, you will want to drink yourself dry.
Drink until you cry the sight from your eyes. Drink until the voices in your head say 'live'.

'Live, live, live because if you don't you won't know life'.

If you don't know life what is there to know but death? That will take you over and all the Hindu sages will laugh because you have lost. You are now just mortal.

Jonny thought that he would live forever, so he walked to the ends of the earth because he had time. There he met a man he could trust, called him brother, leant him his heart and his hand, until one day he woke to find his brother gone. In his place there was just a note that said, *'Live. Live, live, live. Because if you don't you wont know life'.* Jonny remembered the voices he knew people heard and he stepped outside. There he saw the street where he grew up, the primary school where he was taught to read, the lamppost under which he first kissed Holly the day Dylan released Time out of Mind. He saw his driveway, his garden, his house, and his family, unchanged and smiling, because the end of the earth isn't always that far from home.

A sage once whispered the end is when you can hear only the sound of your own breathing and within that, hear music.

I heard music once, so I turned back for home. There I found my sister turned on her head reading Nietzche and laughing. The whole world turned on its head, my sister's five, but she knows more about Good & Evil than I do. She won't cry, she just walks away and every time she does I believe that she's immortal.

Like Jonny she wears her heart on her sleeve and her soul around her wrist. She wants our surname tattooed around her wedding ring finger so that even when she's married she'll be the same immortal girl.

Jonny thought that he would live forever and you could see it when you looked at him that something somewhere out there made sense because Jonny saw it and he held onto it so tight it became a part of him. He heard it calling to him like it would die without him. Jonny responded to that call because he had time. The sort of time that mortals waste on farewells and promises but Jonny never said goodbye.

Jonny thought that he would live forever, but in trying, Jonny died.

SARANGNI

They burst blackberries like bubbles
on the roofs of their mouths.
Sugar-rushed and ripe as a first kiss.
Black tongued, bitter-as-bitter
she watched him wince
and blew him raspberries.

He, berry-lost and brambled,
squashed the final fruit between
finger and thumb
and drew a heart on her palm.
Something caught like a thorn.

That night she refused to wash it off
and woke the next day alone,
stained,
a faint outline of a purple heart
on her chest.

BONES

This life is a bonfire of yesterdays —
it's a tried and tested method
of losing our ways
among the streets of this city we love.
But it's the same sky above;
same as it's always been
the only thing that will listen to your eyes scream
when the slow walkers and fast talkers get a hold of you
but there is more to this city that we wander through,
more to the houses and the homes.
And it's you, city, you're the one who shaped me —
drew lay-lines on my bones and sang lullabies to me —
when the rain fell, we laughed in it;
and when the sun shone, we danced in it;
and when we stood on top of that tower to watch the sun set
we saw the light splash down making the leaves wet.

It's a different thing to look down on what you love;
it's a different thing to be above it all
tracing maps from where you first fell in love
to where you went to school,
but it's a world we all should know:
where the heart beats fast and your eyes blink slow.
It's the paradise we dream of finding;
it's the burning world beyond the horizon
where everything is as it's meant to be
and nothing can hurt you,
nothing can hurt me.
Though we're just strangers,
that doesn't mean I don't love you
because the same fire that burns in me burns in you too.
I can see it, when you look directly at me.
Catch the falling light soaking the trees we stand above.
You remember what I said about love?

It's in the city I grew up in.
It's in the people I've watched growing
into human beings I could cling to,

when the rain sets in I'll give shelter to,
but if you should just find my skeleton picked clean as stones,
you'll find a map of Bristol etched upon my bones.

Lead me to the edge. Let's dare each other to fall
because a life not lived properly
that's not a proper life at all,
and we owe it to the stars, you know,
we owe it to the moon,
because they're the ones who're watching us
dancing through the room.
This life is fleeting,
this life is brief,
but it's fear of these two facts
that people get so scared about
they wind up calling belief.
Me? I'm just a traveller,
with dust upon my shoes,
because you can walk forever
when you've nothing left to lose,
and age is just what happens when you live a life so full
that when you stop to look at time
you realise you've no time at all.

But this city will always cradle me,
from my first love to my last,
from the day I realised the world could change
to standing up here on this stage
watching prophecies come to pass.
It's not a devil that I'm dancing with
it's the sound of my mother's voice,
teaching me the rights and wrongs,
all the words to all the songs,
and that you always have a choice.
And to some that might sound scary
because it's the way you change your life;
to realise there's just two things you can't prevent:
the tide and the night.

And the night is already here now,
you can see it shot full of stars,
so I'll walk down to the beach alone
leave behind the sound of cars.
And the stars reflect in the water,
my father always told me they're the moon's sons
and the sun's daughters
and I don't burn as bright as them,
that's just not the way that I was born,
so, I'll flip a coin in the sand,
fix up how I'm torn between staying here or going
back to the city I love
where I can walk the familiar streets
with demons below and angels above.
And the fates can stand on every corner,
fixing me with a stare,
I'll just drop my eyes and walk on by,
cover my ears to the distant screams and the muffled prayers.

I don't have much for you,
but I can promise you one thing:
if you look for me on the beach, I'll show you the tide
bright and sparkling;
if we look up we'll see the clouds begin to turn;
and if we wait for long enough we'll see the horizon burn;
but when you get there,
if you should just find my skeleton,
picked clean as stones,
you'll find a map of Bristol etched upon my bones.

CONKERS

Even though I know it's true what people say,
that love's just a game,
it's one that I'm too afraid to play.

See, I knew this girl once
who always said her favourite light
was the twice-tricked and rum-golden twilight
that came slowly with the falling leaves
red-wine and open-fire evenings of September.

Her eyes flamed when she looked at me.

It was in one of those evenings that we climbed quietly
into the slow world and chaos of the crows,
where the wine glowed like fire in our glasses
and the trees moved with the sound of our breathing.

And from high on the roof all Bristol lay before us,
we watched worlds collide
in catastrophic beauty
as our own lives fell into step like
Romeo and Juliet
but with a happy ending…

In the distance two kids chased each other
through shadows that bit at their heels,
stealing conkers from the grass
and shooting them into the twilight,
turning and tumbling
leaves and embered hours
wrapped warm in the last few rays of a summer
too soon forgotten.

We raised our glasses.
Drank to them.

She exhaled,
said candles burn brightest when no one is watching
so we turned from those kids to feel the flames burn brighter

at our backs
I put us in their shoes and we ran like them.
We laughed, shot conkers,
built bonfires in the forests of our breasts,
chased fireflies and futures,
with hand-held happiness and hope
before everything burst.
All Bristol lay before us like a blanket we could fall in to.
With all the quiet
and all the noise
condensed into this one moment
of child-like assurance
where we knew nothing of the flames in her eyes
or the fires in our wine —
as on the skyline two figures raised their glasses to us.

We were too tied and trapped in that heavy second
to know then what was blissful foolishness
and what was foolish bliss.
And one of our incarnations kissed.

But time set to wearing the skin of that twilight
smoke thin
before it burnt away.
I'm left to wonder: what will become of us now?
What will become of us when the leaves turn
and the twice-tricked and rum-golden twilight
fills my wine glass with fire?

On those evenings, I climb back to that slow world
and I raise my glass higher.
Drink to those children,
and wonder that,
for that brief moment,
we were just two kids
shooting conkers
into the twilight.

DOG

I have not chased a black dog in so long.
My own dog, whose bright eyes
will always tell me I'm home,
I have chased her.

I have chased her through streets and fields,
woods where I would sleep and breathe
if the days did not chase me too.

And I did it to know how she feels,
to be so free of worry, charging
four-paw and stick-lead through
fields ploughed fresh as February,
with my breath grey and clear
against the morning, night, and the half-light,
and the shadows
dancing in between.

Four years ago I lived because of my dog's eyes.
The night I finished the vodka and the pills,
and sat beside her to say goodnight,
she looked at me as if to say
the only command she knew,
'Stay'.

I lived.
For her and for the chase
through mornings blue as eyes
over hedgerows thick
and heavy with fruit I picked as a child —
from where
on spring-bright Saturdays
my sister and mother and I
would collect caterpillars to watch flutter
come summer.

But the black dog — whose mongering eyes
I have seen in my sleep, and who has,
on nights I shut out of my mind,

breathed darkness into my ears —
still haunts me, quiet as light.

And, though I have not stopped
to chase it away like I did —
though I can still hear its paws
on the grass beneath my window —
I know if I were to turn
I would find it gone.
A shadow
and some paw-prints maybe
but no dog. No darkness.

And that is the only light I need.

STORMS

She's magpies tattooed on her back
and she always longs for the sea.
Comforted by wave and water.
Blue-eyed as storms
rain-iris,
lightning flash and thunder in her smile,
she says the water is her only answer.

On the days when her stories don't add-up,
and the only alibi is her eyes
bolt-bright against the nights,
she waits to hear the clock strike for the witching hour,
when the clouds spread over the moon like a sail,
to steal out to the sea —
gentle first down the yawning streets
that crawl like spiders' webs from her branches.
When she feels the weight of the day pressing
pennies against her eyelids
she sets out faster.

Fast as faithful and full-force to the shore,
past the empty letter-boxes and the curtained windows,
past the sleeping cats and the purring couples
caught love-held and creeping in the half-light.
Past the shops and shutters,
drains and gutters,
parks littered peaceful with mornings.

Streets give way to sand
and her tidal wave keeps building.
Her lungs salt-aired and boundless,
the lighting flashing in her eyes,
her hair wave-tossed and dark
against the fading light of the town.

Deep and cold,
breathless against the tide
spinning each wave against her cheek,

she swims until her feet don't touch the bed,
smiling like she is home.

In all the tossing ocean,
of sea salt and sand and sail,
one girl swims alone against the tide.
Mad as moonlight,
tempestuous,
storms held between her teeth,
the ocean is her only lullaby.

Like a boat tacked against the wind she rocks,
storm held and wave tossed,
brave as bold and brittle as bones
her relief crashes on the shore.

SHIPPING

You know what I want to be when I grow up? I want to be the man who reads the shipping forecast. The man who talked me to sleep as a child like a father and the same voice that echoed through my true father's ears each night: *Dogger, Fisher, German Bight.*

The sea song singing to the waves of radio and water we drift through this life like life-rafts with no warnings of good or poor. And I wonder if the pain I felt when my first love left me could have been averted by the reports of the sea. Or if the day the real world hit me like an ocean liner it would have mattered so much less if I'd known of backwards, veering, storms and poor-ness. Most of all, I think of the day I picked up the phone to the sound of my mother's tears singing to me like a storm and lashing my lighthouse cheek, and I wonder, would word of good visibility in Lundy have soothed me any?

The day Bert Jansch died my father and I sat in silence and listened to every song of his we had. Over and over we played them and never spoke and it was one of those moments of beauty and brutality that cling to you like fog and seaweed and you cradle them — keep them in your heart — think only of them when you wake up shivering in the dark wondering when the light of morning will reach you once again. Like every night before bed when the words of the seas hypnotise me like chanting: *The time is 12.48, and now for the Shipping Forecast.*

And somewhere out there, maybe Biscay, veering south four or five, rain, poor. How close can we sail to the storm? How close can we get to the eye of life before we break up and drown? Shoot flares up when I leave, brighten the bay, but you need only listen to the sounds of the radio to know I have not left you; I will still be there to soothe you to sleep each night. Whatever, whenever, wherever I go the voice on the radio soothes me like everything is fair and clear, veering six or seven eastwards to the rising sun and outwards to the place where the seas are always calm.

And these days we sail like Rockall — tempestuous but beautiful and always with fair warning of our dreams.

The day my father leaves me for the last time I will listen for word of Fitzroy and Sole and imagine it is his voice I hear telling me everything will be fair and clear. Maybe that might bring me some comfort from the world, even if only for 10 minutes before I sleep, like a bedtime story that never changes but keeps you cradled in its arms.

So, you ask why it is my dream to read you these words? This poem of the smallest seas. I answer: every night that voice makes me feel like nothing will be poor or moderate, but only good and when we veer, we veer towards the light and the brightness and the place where the world is warmer; the winds may blow but they blow to take us back to where we need to be; though the rain may fall, it falls to remind us to smile more when the sun shines.

Why wouldn't you want to be that poet, who reads the patterns of the winds and knows the rhyme and reason of the rain, and in doing so brings comfort to the hearts of all those who hear? He is the voice of your father when your father is not there. So, I will be the voice to soothe you to sleep each night: *The time is 12.48, and now for the shipping forecast.*

And somewhere, out there, in North Utsire, South Utsire, backwards, three or four westwards, blow me home now and take me in the arms of my city. Tell me everything is clear.
Though I know back home a storm is brewing as I sit awake into night waiting for the Faeroes to be fair and for those ten minutes when I know of Malin, Hebrides, Bailey and can finally rest my head. Until, one day, when you sail too close to the storm, turn your ears to me and I will be the voice of your father telling you that everything is fair and clear:
The time is 12.48, and now for the shipping forecast…

CATHY

There's this girl haunting my memory
scrawling promises on the inside of my mind
like prophesies.
The first time we had sex I bit her,
so hard I left a scar on her lip
— like a story.
I did it
half out of passion
half out of a need to hurt her.
I know it reminds her
of the night our blood stepped out and danced,
hands up to the sky like a supernova
we became each other.
Same body, same soul.
I said, 'This.
This will be the death of me.'
She laughed.
She always loved morbidity.

That night,
I was 23,
I was standing patiently
watching the high-heeled girls drift listlessly
through the darkening streets
then she…
she looked like a dream to me.
With champagne eyes and cigarette lips
I hungered to kiss.
We played a fools game.
Started from scratch with just a name.
But we were the eternal rocks beneath.
Not a source of delight but necessary;
we had no choice but to be.

That night we held the city to ransom,
she called me handsome,
knowing I was hers all the same,
and when she kissed me I nearly…

skipped a heartbeat.
Watched the pavement pass from under our feet.

She cocked a pistol pressed it to my temple,
nothing is ever simple, she said.
In a metaphor we never needed,
I still believed it.
That something in the barrel-steel
lead me to it;
is what makes me lie to her
and lie with her.

With each kiss bursting on our lips like chilli flakes
we stayed up late.
In the morning I stroked her face
like a cat playing with a mouse.
When we left her house
she clenched her fists and looked down
when we talked of plans.
Wincing like I was biting.
When she wasn't listening I called her Cathy.
I knew that when I slept she called me Heathcliff,
saying, 'Whatever our souls are made of,
his and mine are the same.'

She promised then to haunt me,
not leave me alone in this abyss.
Now her eyes stalk the shadows inside my head
I wish I could hold her until we both were dead,
but that's too easy for us.
Too easy to just fade out,
not burn like stars or eyes.

She'll always be a wild thing. A changeling.
A warrior I drew blood from
on a night I wish I didn't remember so vividly.
That first night we made love,
the last time I saw her,
before she came to haunt me like she promised.

EINAUDI

Einaudi was ours.
Though this held no more truth than saying
we owned the stars,
the moon and Mars.
For one night, perhaps,
we did hold them closer than others.
Mothers and lovers the world over
watched the lights fade,
as our arms wrapped full around the bodies
quick as evening.

At dawn yawning we rubbed sleep from our eyes —
Einaudi playing quietly into a waking room —
rose and walked into the day.
Piano key footsteps ringing in our ears
and in our palms
moon dust. Just enough
to remind us of the night
the moon was ours
and to carry us through
the day like dancers.

HOME

These things I know I count on my bones
laid out like stones on a river bed,
washed clean and smooth, graceful
among the stone trees of my orchard.

Climbing high and easy, I ran
through skies blue and bright as a fuse,
chased sparks like kittens and kites,
with bright lights and stars and the sun
dancing across my eyes like a drum.

The veins of my forearms
pumped with my Bristol-born blood,
pulsating like dancing streets,
weak only when the music stops,
and the city's silence overcomes me.

Me, whose eyes you can trace
from the basin to Clifton,
past the parks I ran through when,
young as I have been,
I caught matches between my teeth.

And on the tower top, look out.
You'll see my initials
scratched against the sky,
my lasting token to the city that raised me.

My love letter:
Sealed with a nod to the stars that watched,
the scribbled writing my mother gave me
illegible as eye-lids but loving.

We made it, City,
and I hold your streets to me like veins.

UNTITLED

the words itched like a phantom limb
and I longed to scratch
to dig my fingernails ink-deep
and fill this room empty
not with words but their presence
the weight of things whispered
said, unsaid and sung
the dark matter of our dreams
that consume us
smoke-filled and choking
until the alarm rings and we forget

the door creaked ajar
the itch flared for a moment
then stopped
and on the walls
among my scribbles of breathing
I could make out a line that I loved

PUPPET

She called him the shadow puppet boy
the way his hands entwined against the morning sun
above the white sheets they had slept on —
her: heart beating out of its chest;
he: worried his blinking would wake her
from whatever dream kept her jolting.

He carved characters out of darkness,
polished their shoulders and rounded their limbs,
planted voices rich with purpose,
morning-sung and simple.
He fathered them.

The steam rose from their tea as he stretched stories
over the sunlight.
Skipped and trembling
the shadows grew,
leaping before them like children
eager for weekends in the park
or to pillow-fight the day or the dog.

These stories were everything to them —
whispered narratives arching in the drowsy bedroom air.

In the puppet-dark night time
he tried the moon instead. Lamps. Candles. The last match.
The torch his father had lent him
the winter the fuses kept blowing.
But the characters he formed kept failing
empty and lonely
burnt out as stars
or old fuses.

So they slept instead. And in the morning
she called him the shadow puppet boy
as they entwined their hands
soft and dark against the morning sun.

BRISTOL

Each day we grow we go toe-to-toe with living
and that drags me out of bed.
I think of something I read somewhere once:
that there was a time
when your parents picked you up and held you
then put you down
and never picked you up again.

Imagine how difficult
if you knew that was happening.

I think of that every day because I miss my home
the faces I know, knew, loved.
The cider-weathered gardens,
sun-swept, lip-whip-kissed where the city meets the sea;
Gloucester Road, Downs and basin,
where you can hear the city sing.

And I think.

One day I will drive away,
Graceland dancing on the radio,
the sun shining cider-apple white,
and Bristol slowly fading out.

I'll never see her again.

A leaf will fall in a park somewhere,
a boy will stand before a girl
kiss her shame-shy where the sky sings quietest —
just like I did once —
and no one will ever be able to point to the moment
I left. Not even me.

She won't think of me too often,
only when it rains.
but we'll both know there was a time we stopped kissing
and never started again.

I hope the city that bore me,
saw me sing and soar high as heaven-held
will pause for a moment
just to watch time passing.
They'll be singing in the streets for the first day of summer,
the stars as flowers in their eyes,
mothers the city over holding their children tight,
lovers with kisses in their hands,
and me. Driving.
Bristol fading into the tears
slowly filling my eyes.

And I'll never see her again.

INSOMNIA

What keeps you awake at night?

Me? I'm kept awake by the wub and thud of blood upon flesh and echoes of emotion that you and I convince ourselves comes from the same organ that keeps the tears pumping round our veins.

And I'm sick of it.

I want to step forward and step out and step up into the sky like *Unfinished Sympathy*; with the ones I love living below me, to fly with them, to cry with them
and, even though I've no more power,
I'm no God,
they can be safe in the knowledge that someone is watching over them and that he cares.

Because I do care
I care so much it keeps me awake at night
I just wanted you to know that.

There's a tree across the street
time-old and still growing like a sapling.
In the sun-hung blue-sky days you can hear it
laughing all acorns and boughs.
In the night-time you can hear it cry.
And if I have to spend one more night under
the same sky never sleeping
I'll be stood there with it
crying too.

Some nights I'm kept awake by the deafening emotion
of the girl who sleeps beside me,
who kisses me in the darkness and
whispers something I am always too stunned to hear
though I know sounds a lot like love.

People count sheep to get to sleep,
but not me.
I string my words together
and hang them like Christmas lights
not because I believe in what they stand for
but because it looks good.

Some nights I'm kept awake by the sound of my own heart
beating like a stopwatch
and I set to thinking how long I will go,
where I'll end up,
and my life maps out before me like a comic strip
but all I can focus on is the frame I stand in now…

I don't want to know the name of the girl I'll marry,
I just want to know what she looks like
so I know I won't miss her.

I don't want to know how the world will end,
with a bang or a whimper,
I just want to know someone will be standing there with me.

Most of all I just want to know there's a story at all.

So tonight I'm going to read one more chapter,
put one more piece in the puzzle,
tonight and the next night.
And the moon will shine just as bright,
the stars will burn just as fierce,
the tree across the street will cry so loud all acorns and boughs
that my head will split in two and the girl who sleeps beside
me will be deafened by the rush,
but tonight
I just want to sleep
I just want to rest.
Tonight, I just want to dream.

ONCE

Make love to me,
like I am the best of all the bad mistakes you'll make this week.

Cry wolf,
when the grey-flecked beast of your night lies down before you.

Speak slowly,
like every word should be savoured on the tip of your tongue.

Watch closely,
when the shadows show all the things you still long to do.

Write gently,
because a misplaced word can run from you like a beast.

Sing once,
any more than once and you lose feeling from each breath.

Break a promise,
so you know how it feels to break someone and learn.

Love hard,
because it should hurt.

It should hurt until you have nothing left to give.

GRAFFITI

The girl who lives at the end of my road just skipped town.
She took with her a suitcase full of shoes,
a picture of herself when she was 14,
and a man who wears a clown mask
just to hide the tears she makes him cry.

Some people truly don't give a fuck about the world
and she's one.
I once watched her drop a duffle full of pennies down
a wishing well
and with each drop…
she would wish that she were dead.

You could see it when you looked at her
that something inside her didn't sit right with the world
didn't sit right with a world that cared more about her
than she would ever care to admit.
She always curled her lip when said goodbye
and even though she was a model
you've never met anyone so ugly.

There's graffiti on the walls says,
"I have fallen in love tonight".
The saddest thing?
I think she wishes she wrote it.

Instead she has to look on
with the same wishing-well loathing
she shouldn't have had to get used to.
She should know how soft her skin is;
she shouldn't have to be reminded by the metal of a blade
how soft her skin is.
There's a song I love
about a girl with depression
whose parents put a mirror in her bedroom.
They made her smile at it three times a day
and it drove her depression away.

I gave her a mirror,
to see what she saw.
Hours passed before I finally plucked up the courage
to ask her why she stared.
She said,
"I just want to know what this mirror looks like,
because to me it looks like the black water of a wishing well
and smells like the melodies of songs
about far off places".
I don't think she meant me to see her cry.

There's graffti on the walls says,
"I have fallen in love tonight".
The saddest thing?
I think she wishes she wrote it.

Instead she scrawls on her breast with eye-liner
"Stay out of my dreams, you know who you are."
But I don't think that person does know.

The man in the clown mask wishes it was him.
A little bit of me wishes it was me,
and maybe a little piece of you wishes it was you
because what greater recognition
than to be loved by someone who cannot love.

"I have fallen in love tonight"
is scrawled in six foot high letters on the wall
and someone, please, come clean.
Tell me what they mean.

She thinks it's a simple equation
of cause and effect,
but I know a penny in a well won't change the world.

The man with the clown mask scrawls on
the inside of Dorian Gray
"I'm not here to be the hero; I just want to save you from yourself".

He keeps leaving it lying around
in the hope she might read it
and take note,
but it's been nine months and still nothing
has been born of his efforts
and he's beginning to wonder
when he should of stopped.
He doesn't need me to tell him.

It was after their first date,
when they walked down the middle of the road
smoking Gauloise and drinking red wine from the bottle.
When she kissed him and read graffiti on the walls that said,
"I have fallen in love tonight".
And the saddest thing?

The wall was blank.

KETTLE

Only once have I fallen asleep
without whispering your name
or remembering
the way you recited my poems back to me
like I had written them with your tongue.

It was the day we watched Twelfth Night
in the park beside my house —
remembering suddenly
the revenges brought in.
And returning sun-burned
we held each other until the kettle boiled.

You left before I had poured the milk
or dropped a sugar-lump
chiming into your favourite mug.

FOXES

Woken by the scream of foxes fucking
in the garden beneath our window
you reached for me.

The garden we looked down on
pretending it was ours
on warm evenings when we smoked
from the window waiting
for autumn.

The foxes fucked full throttle and barking.
We were Seraphim
above the chaos
as we ground our bones together.

I prayed for us.
So hard I thought I heard a god cry out —
a cry so like a vixen's.

Our heaven was shrinking
in the global warming of our sheets —
nature undone.
Tomorrow's cups of tea, skimmed milk and one sugar,
black coffee I stained my tongue with.

I am not the man you think I am.
I can be neither human nor fox for you.

FOOL

In a world where the lines are bleeding someone needs to patch up the wound. But it's not me.

I wish I could see. See what I feel and why. Because I'm so lost in the cracks between the definitions, between blurred lines and half rhymes someone keeps telling me need patching up like a wound.

Hit the bar, drink while you can, do it for me. Mine's a double whisky. I'll raise my glass to you at the back because I bet you got some stories to tell. I wonder if they might fill the void that used to be a pin-hole — used to be a pin hole until I got nervous and picked at it, stripped it out and made it gape, faked a belief that all good things shall come to pass, a belief that good guys don't finish last.

But it's just you and me now. You think you can take that?
I can't promise I'll make you sing, but I'll do my best to make you smile though it may take a while. Because I'm still lost in the cracks between the definitions of you and me. You see, it's dark up here. Metaphorically…

You will never feel more alone than when you're confronted with bright lights hiding the faces of an audience whose intentions you can never be sure of. Audiences who listen intently as you stumble through the words that when you shouted them at your mirror with such verve you thought, yeh, that'll work. You'll never feel more alone than when you forget those words.

And it's a kind of premature pathetic fallacy when it's already raining before you've even taken the mic. When out there there's a storm raging in the street and a man in a cloak, a clown mask, in the dark daring to breathe in the bitter air that will let him speak, *'Blow winds and crack your cheeks'*. And there's graffiti on the walls by his side, but the only word I can make out is *'tonight'*. Like, deep in him, and scrawled across the Dorian Gray wall there's a fight taking hold and he's soon to turn break-heeled and tripping through the darkening streets with my words echoing after him like an elegy to one who truly believed that all good things come to pass and nice guys don't finish last. But, for all this blind running, he's just one more fool in a storm calling out for a king.

You at the back, the guy with the stories, does this sound familiar?

I wish I could blunt the edges of this story so I might not cut myself on them. They're razor sharp dangling too close to my heart, reflecting my eyes, reflecting my meanings, and deep down there's a king, weary in a storm, a cracked crown and a tattered gown, and a painted smile like a clown.

There's graffiti on the walls at the back of my mind but the only word I can make out is *'tonight',* and the king in me is too tired to fight, too weary to figure out what may and what might. Drowning in the flooded cracks between the definitions of king and clown, painted face or regal gown. I wonder what the man in the clown mask might make of this, because he knows more than most about the fine line between human and ghost and the definitions of both.

If we listen carefully, we might just hear in the streets outside and just reaching our ears a whisper that comes past the closed shops and the padlocks, past the window lights and the winds that blow and bite and I think I can make out what it says. I think I can make out what it says because it's the same words I sometimes let fall: *"This cold night will turn us all to fools and madmen."* Now I'm the fool.

So buy up and drink up, lets listen to the man with the stories, he's been where I am now, succeeding in a way I don't think I can. So this is where I'll stay; it's where I'll swim and some day, when I reach the shores of understanding, it'll be where I stand: a king and a fool. It's just who I am.

LONELY

Take heart from the friends that flock to you;
who carry your books and brush your hair;
who wipe tears from your cheeks;
make endless cups of milk and sugared tea
and agree with you that life isn't fair.
Take heart from those who love you —
there are so many, too many to count
surrounding you.

You have watched, I know, the life you chose
wither before you.
Your hands clutch at cloudless days,
the sun does not worry you,
but a blue sky is like air to embers.

Remembering is painful and easy.
As birds sitting restless
on the branches by our window,
your thoughts tremble.

A man, young as I, a boy
in my own eyes
can offer so little to the driftwood and kindling of your bones,
but what little I hold is nothing
to the flames in my fingers
as I run them through your hair
and brush tears from your cheeks.

So, when clouds cover you,
and the restless pain of knowing
threatens to consume you,
look up,
and I will drink the clouds dry,
so you,
lovely and lonely,
love of all,
can see only blue sky.

FOOTPRINTS

In the hallways I see footprints
dug into the deep carpet where the flowers
bloomed from thread.

The words came quicker then —
slippery and electric on my tongue as eels —
and you stood there and watched the evening
light up like lightening from my lips.

I saw in your eyes that you were too afraid to kiss me
for fear of being so shocked you could not pull away.

A man strange as I,
eyes fixed as sapphires,
wanted you to reach across the halls
and leave footprints once more.

When I look now I see the flowers still blooming
though the footprints have long died out.

DYLANS

Caitlin Thomas said that when Dylan died all she could hear in the sound of the train-wheels back to Laugharne was 'no Dylan, no home, no Dylan, no home, no Dylan, no home'...

I heard train wheels in your voice the day you cupped your
chin in your hands like a vice and said to me:
'I'm jealous of every person on this earth who is yet to know
what it feels like to meet you for the first time'.
When your eyes flashed blue like an ambulance light and my
fingers reached out to push three nines on the telephone
just to be certain that someone was rushing to save me.

Then a flat line beep that faded out like a heart.

And a whisper.

That day the summer finally came for us
I left the Bob Dylan LP you gave me
leaning against the red door I closed
when the paramedics left.
When I stopped by last week, there was no Dylan
there any more and the door had ceased to feel like home.

No Dylan, no home.

So, I hid my whistles between pavement cracks
knowing when you stepped on them you'd be reminded of me.
I left my breathing in the trees,
so one breeze could take you back to lying beside me as I sleep.
And I left my last shot at absolution, folded neatly and hidden.
I know you'll find it soon.

Look carefully at the patch of skin where your elbow bends;
I still love, it says, *for all my sins.*

There are and will always be days when I will look up to the
clouds to see if I can't make out your name in the god rays that
come streaming through them like dancers.
But in those moments the only hands I have to hold are on my

watch face,
spinning away from me with each second I don't get to hold your body against mine.

Not everyone wants to go home, some people just want to feel safe.

I hope that night you arrived where you had always been trying to go, even if you arrived too late.
But there are no more stars or stories for you now.
No blue eyes in the cigarette smoke.
No hearts or bones or beds or guns.
No back scratched, lip-bitten beautiful embraces to tremble from.
No dogs among the fairies.
No Cathy.
No Dylan. No Home. No Dylan. No Home. No Dylan. No Home…

WRITE

I hope your head will listen,
your heart will eventually lose its voice.
I can hear it holding its breath.
Building up to scream.

I did not know these worlds were parallel.
I thought they would cross eventually.
Cross crucified patiently
though the blood did not flow from me like normal.

My everything, they shouted.
My ever after and my bright beginnings.
We did not keep our promises
and look at where it brought us.

There's a story in your eyes,
I can't read it, but I see it's there
hiding behind your hatred
beside the lightning flash
and the graffiti.
Write it. I'll buy you a pen.
Blue like the one you marked-up my essays with
on Wednesdays in the library
when we told the world we were studying only.

I would give you the last piece of paper on this earth
if you swore on your skull you wouldn't write me on it.
The things you did in those years,
those lavish years, those habits,
should never be repeated in fact or fiction.

We all make mistakes,
I think you just thought you had a talent for it.
No one asked to be here,
but here is where we are.
Let's make a night of it.
I brought some stories —
cut the crusts off
but they're delicious

if that's what you're in to.
Like loaves and fishes we'll deal them out,
amongst the faithful and the faithless.

Build up the barricade.
Hang out the dirty laundry.
Write the letter you never meant to send
then nail it to the church door at midnight.
These crossroads were not dug deep with skeletons.
Those dancers aren't dancing they're lost —
And, all-in and over, we will clap when the house lights dim.

Wish me well the night you leave
because deeper than any water I will not see your smile again
this lifetime.
Maybe next time around.

I hope we meet again,
I do,
just don't remember this.
Goodbyes become bittersweet
when people like us remember them.
It's easy to get lost in the gaps between words —
I just wish that was a valid excuse,
something there's a pill for.

Tell me when the story is done,
I'd like to read it.
Just to be safe.

SENSE

When déjà vu becomes something new,
when steady hands tremble white and shake,
your eyes will be the sense to hold you true.

Eyes rain-iris and Bristol-bottle blue
so fragile they may crack each time you wake.
When déjà vu becomes something new.

When lips, red lips, whose kisses knew so few
that when they part to breathe they also make
the taste of breath the sense to hold you true.

All and over, they still remember you,
songs sound as sea-shores, still as lakes,
when déjà vu becomes something new.

Breathe in, know autumn seeping through
the photographs and memories that you take
to drink come spring, the sense to hold you true.

But you no longer walk the streets you knew.
Your eyes flash, hide how deep you ache
when déjà vu becomes something new
and you call for any sense to hold you true.

JULY

July crept on me like darkness. Wrapped
its tongue around mine and pulled me close.
Pressed heart-close and closed,
lip-whipped and passionless,
then fled from me easy as easy
and breathing. Breathless, but breathing.

The grass where we'd waited was pressed.
Browning, dying and drying. I,
still as prey, made no sense, nor tried.
And when the street-light burst,
moved only to blink.
Once, like a whip-crack, then still again.

In the open-ended evening someone
pressed their hand to my palm,
kneaded the blood back to my fingers
like paste. Splashed rain on my eyes
and as the picture focused they broke
clouds upon my ear drums, hushed
and wave-soft. Gently then. Gentle.

PHOTOGRAPHS

Tracing thoughts across the sky like conkers,
we move so slowly the time turns backwards with us.
The silver you wear around your neck is the only thing that tells the future.

Amongst the cloud-counting and the hidden stars
there are memories so fragile they could shatter at the thought of a stone,
and we carry them like wings through the flute-gaps in the trees.

That time we drank wine from the bottle,
and took photographs in black and white,
was where it all focused.
I know, if we stay here long enough,
the time moving backwards will eventually reach that point and stop,
too afraid to see what would happen
if it was erased.
Those black and white images,
that one black and white image I held closer than any other
because you could still make out the blue of your iris
and the torture in your smile.

We always revert to the chaos,
watch the world sink.
You were always the stronger swimmer.

Tomorrow, I'm going back to that.
I'm going back to where we started it all with a green rose,
the conker you kept on your windowsill,
the book of Blake we read by the lake,
the Dylan LP,
the mug you painted a storm in.
The smiles that knew nothing of the future and the fire.
Next time around, I won't question it
I'll just live it.

Next time, I'll write this all like a story.

THANKS AND ACKNOWLEDGEMENTS

Thanks to Thommie Gillow and Clive Birnie for the hours of work that have gone into creating this book and for remaining patient and eternally encouraging. To my mother for instilling a love of literature in me. My father for introducing me to Dylan Thomas and Bob Dylan, whose writing has influenced me more than any other. My sister, Cat, for years of sustained teasing and support. My best friends JR and MacKenzie, on whose shoulders I have leant so many times. Sarah Karmali for being my anchor however calm or stormy the seas. Chris McCafferty, in whose house these poems were finally shaped into a book. The team behind Acoustic Night Bristol for giving me a mic at the start. Buddy Wakefield for setting me on the journey. Bohdan Piasecki for his guidance in the early days. All the promoters who have ever booked me and the audiences who have ever watched and listened to me. Luke Kennard, Dan Cockrill, and Sally Jenkinson for the kind words about Conkers. My secondary school English teachers, Kelvin Furze and Cressida Inglis. And finally to Bristol. Everything starts and ends with Bristol.

www.ingramcontent.com/pod-product-compliance
Lightning Source LLC
Chambersburg PA
CBHW021000090426
42736CB00010B/1401